# The Mystery of JACK the One-Eyed Kitten

## A True Story

Jeanette E. Lewis

ISBN 978-1-957943-77-0 (paperback)
ISBN 978-1-957943-78-7 (hardback)
ISBN 978-1-957943-79-4 (digital)

Rushmore Press LLC
1 800 460 9188
www.rushmorepress.com

Printed in the United States of America

# FINDING JACK

One chilly February day, Jan and her friend Jane decided to go to lunch after they finished bowling.* After eating at a restaurant, Jan went to buy cat food, as she had quite a few cats at home, so she headed to the pet store and took a shortcut behind the shopping center. While driving, Jan saw a little brown something that looked like a kitten lying on the concrete near a store. She continued on to the pet store because she could hardly believe her eyes. How could a little kitten get there? After shopping for her cats, Jan went back to check on the kitten. Yes, there it was, looking very unhappy and cold, a little brown kitten! Jan parked her car and went over to the kitten which seemed sick, barely alive and abandoned.** Jan saw two men who worked for the shopping center and she asked them if they had any gloves. They did, and gave them to Jan so she could put the kitten in a small box she just happened to have in her car.

---

* bowling is an indoor sport in which people aim a heavy ball at ten pins at the end of a wooden alley, hoping to knock them all down.
** abandoned means to have no one to care for you.

# JACK VISITS THE VET

Jan drove directly to the veterinarian's* office so she could find out what was wrong with the little brown kitten. He was very ill, the veterinarian said: he had a very bad cold which gave him a bad odor, a bulging eye which the vet said would have to be removed, and the other eye was cloudy. He weighed only one and half pounds but was already shedding his baby teeth. The vet said he had not had enough food and probably that was why his fur was brown, not black, and dry. The poor little kitten was almost blind. The vet gave the little brown kitten some medicine and gave Jan some medicine to take home for him.

---

\* A veterinarian is a doctor for animals

# JACK COMES HOME

Jan took the little brown kitten home and made him comfortable in her extra bathroom so he would not make her other cats sick. He was so very hungry and thirsty! He immediately learned to use his litter box*, and purred whenever Jan came to pet him and give him his medicine. Because he was so sick he slept a lot. But then, Jan had to go away to another town because her mother was having an operation and Jan was needed to help, so she hired** Donna to feed all of her cats, including the little brown kitten.

---

\* a litter box is a bathroom for cats
** "hired" means to pay someone

# JACK'S EYE FALLS OUT

Jan's husband had been giving Jack his medicine, but suddenly he also had to go into the hospital while Jan was away tending to her mother in the hospital. When Donna came to feed the cats, she discovered to her horror that Jack's bulging eye had fallen out! She had never seen anything like it. It was decided that she should take the kitten to the animal emergency room, which she did. Because things were very complicated at Jack's house, Jan called her daughter Jenny, who lived in another town, to come home to help her daddy and Jack. So she did. Jenny took Jack from the emergency clinic to his regular veterinarian where he had his dangling eye removed, and his eyelids sewn together. He looked like he was winking all the time. And this is when he was named Jack, after the one-eyed Jack in a deck of cards.* How much would Jack be able to see with his one cloudy eye?

---

\* a deck of cards are playing cards used for card games.

# JACK WEARS A CONE

After surgery, it is usual for pets to wear an Elizabethan collar or a cone, which goes around their neck and keeps them from licking their wound. Part of cats' grooming rituals are to lick their paws and rub their faces with them to clean themselves. So Jack could not touch his face because of his eye stitches. Jan wondered how he would eat, but he managed because he had a very good appetite. She would clean his cone when it got dirty. Neither his cone nor being almost blind kept him from being a normal kitten, like playing with his jingle bell ball. He loved to chase it round and round the bathroom. So Jack seemed to have some vision.

Finally, Jack had healed enough to get his cone off and he was a happy cat, except that he still had a little cold, so it was back to the veterinarian. She gave him some medicine and also some for Jan to give him. It was the perfect medicine because his cold finally went away. Jack had put on weight and his fur was beginning to turn black, so he was a black cat after all. It was also getting shinier. He now had the run of Jan's sewing room, and run he did! He could see well enough to use his kitten energy to run circles around Jan's big sewing table.

# JACK GETS AN X-RAY

One day, Jan returned home to find that Jack could see better than she realized he could. He had found one of her sewing machine bobbins* and was playing with it, batting it around on the floor, its thread untangling around Jack and all over the room. Jan was angry with herself for not putting the bobbin away because she didn't want to endanger Jack in any way and she saw that he had thread in his mouth. She removed it and it didn't seem like he had swallowed any, which would have meant Jack needed surgery** but just to be sure, she took Jack once again to the veterinarian where he had an x-ray. No, Jack had not swallowed any thread.

---

\* a bobbin is a small round disk for the sewing machine
\*\* surgery is an operation in which the doctor cuts the patient open to see inside.

# A LEAP OF FAITH

Now that Jack was completely well, Jan wanted to give him more room than just her sewing room. She opened her sewing room door and out walked Jack. Jan's other cats saw him and when Jack saw them he tried to chase them. So Jan put up a barrier to keep Jack from going beyond this room into the rest of the house. But Jack was a very clever and brave kitten because he figured out that if he climbed onto a bookshelf he could see over the barrier. Eventually, he decided to leap from the book shelf over the barrier to the floor, so he had to be confined back into the sewing room because Jan's other cats were afraid of Jack.

# JACK GOES TO HIS FOREVER HOME

Jan's daughter Jenny had a friend Jennifer who wanted Jack, but she lived a long way from him. So one weekend Jan and her husband, Jack in his cat carrier and all of his things like his ball that lit up when it was batted around, his litter box, cat bowls and kitten food were loaded into the car. After driving all day, they reached Jack's forever home where Jennifer was really excited to have him in her arms. Everyone was anxious about how well Jack would get around Jennifer's apartment because it was new territory to Jack, but he could see well enough to avoid obstacles. Jack loved his new home and his new cat person and she loved him as well. They would sit together on the couch and Jack would chew on Jennifer's hair a little bit while she watched television. However, he was afraid of her little round self-propelled vacuum cleaner and would sit on the back of the couch to watch it from a distance while it cleaned the apartment. For some reason (after all, who can explain what cats are thinking?) he liked to play with the bathroom door. His litter box was in there and he locked himself out of the bathroom one day. Oh, dear, that was not good.

Another adventure Jack had was when a hurricane* came to where Jennifer lived. The wind blew very, very hard and it rained and rained for five days. It was a good thing Jack was an inside cat, not used to going outside. Jennifer and Jack were safe where her apartment was.

_____

\* a hurricane is a huge storm with much wind and rain

# JACK HAS A FAN CLUB

Jack's doctor thinks he has about fifty percent vision in his eye, which explains why he is so daring, but also how he gets into trouble. Fifty percent vision means he can see half of what a normal cat sees out of one eye. He is even brave enough to jump up on Jennifer's counter in the kitchen. Jan is so thankful she picked up the sick, sad little brown kitten who has turned into a handsome, sleek, loving black cat. He is such good company for Jennifer and Jennifer is a good cat mommy to Jack. They are both so very contented. When Jennifer takes Jack to his veterinarian's office everyone wants to pet him and hug him because he has such a happy personality and is now a very big cat, weighing in at over twelve pounds. It is a happy ending for Jack, who started out as such a sick little kitten.

# JACK GETS A FRIEND

While Jennifer was at work one day she and her co-worker were talking about cats and kittens when they heard a mew. Kittens mew and cats meow. Jennifer went to see where the sound was coming from and there was a little kitten just outside her office door at the back of her building. Since the little kitten seemed to be a stray* Jennifer took her home, thinking she would find a home for the kitten. But Jack loved the new kitten, so Jennifer kept her and named her "Kismet" which means "destiny", as if Kismet was meant to be with Jack. Now Kismet and Jack are best friends, and Jennifer and her cats are living happily ever after. But Jan still wonders, and will forever wonder, how Jack came to be lying so sick on the cold concrete at the shopping center, and where was his mother? That is the mystery of Jack.

---

* A stray is an animal that does not have a home.

www.ingramcontent.com/pod-product-compliance
Lightning Source LLC
Chambersburg PA
CBHW041532120626
46551CB00018B/2662